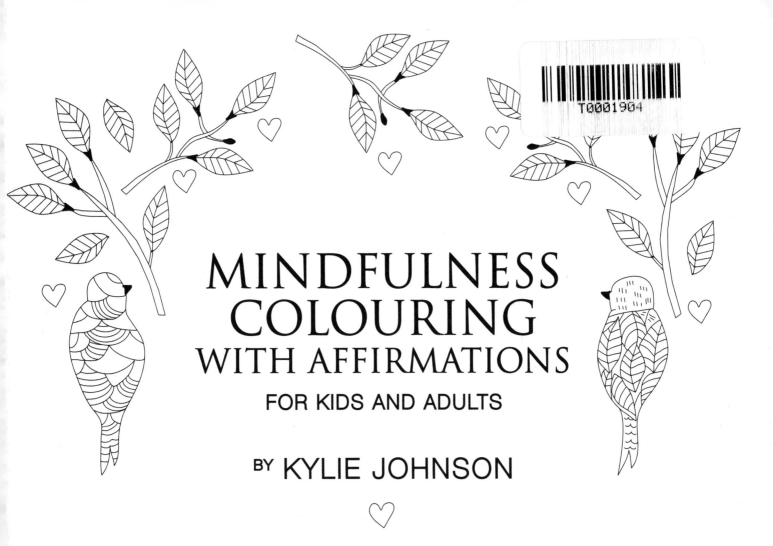

MINDFULNESS COLOURING
WITH AFFIRMATIONS
FOR KIDS AND ADULTS

BY KYLIE JOHNSON

♡

colour your future
with confidence

NH
NEW
HOLLAND

I dedicate this book to
my loving late mother Verna
and grandmother Mardy.

I thank my adoring daughter Jasmin for blessing me
with such love and giving me the gift of motherhood,
for bringing much inspiration into my life.

Published in 2022 by New Holland Publishers
Sydney

Level 1, 178 Fox Valley Road, Wahroonga, NSW 2076, Australia

newhollandpublishers.com

First published in Australia August 2017 by K JJJ Designs Pty Ltd

Copyright © 2022 New Holland Publishers
Copyright © 2022 in text and images: Kylie Johnson

A record of this book is held at the National Library of Australia.

ISBN 9781760795412

Created and Designed by Kylie Johnson

Managing Director: Fiona Schultz
Production Director: Arlene Gippert
Printed in China

10 9 8 7 6 5 4 3 2 1

Keep up with New Holland Publishers:

❦ NewHollandPublishers

◎ @newhollandpublishers

Mindfulness is a key tool that can be used to create the gentle and accepting kind of awareness that bonds a parent and child together. This beautiful book, with affirmations for both adults and kids, will bring peace and colour into your family home. Enjoy!

Professor Lea Waters (PhD)
Gerry Higgins Chair in Positive Psychology

Mindfulness is increasingly referred to as the foundation of a flourishing life. Whilst children naturally appear to be more mindful than adults, there are times when a mindful activity for children can provide a breathing space for both children and parents. There's also increasing scientific support for the use of mindfulness highlighting the significant benefits for both children and adults. Kylie has created a beautiful mindful colouring book with positive affirmations that will encourage children and adults to be more mindful and optimistic and experience an increased sense of calm, which is now more than ever required in our busy lives. My hope is that it will also help families to flourish.

Dr Suzy Green
Clinical & Coaching Psychologist
CEO & Founder of The Positivity Institute

Kylie's Mindful Affirmations Colouring book offers something unique to the known psychological benefits of colouring in, adding the powerful adjunct of affirmations, or positive self talk. My work with children and adolescents has shown how this simple exercise of engaging with a parent/carer in an activity of mindfulness can be hugely beneficial in developing the life skill of emotional regulation. Treat your child, and yourself, to the wonder of mindfulness and the power of positive self talk with this inspirational resource.

Jac Payne (Registered Psychotherapist/Counsellor)
BA (Psych), B Sc (Hons) Psych, MCAP

I love the book that Kylie has created! As a developmental psychologist, I can't emphasise enough the importance of good role-modeling. Children typically don't listen to what we say but watch what we do. How wonderful when we can provide them with tools to help them calm their minds, dealing with stress, to become aware of their inner world and connect with their emotions. Practising mindfulness is a skill that children can easily learn, just like learning how to ride a bike. With these wonderful colouring pages, practising mindfulness together is fun!

Monique Daal, Developmental Psychologist (MSc),
Coach and Author of "No Limit Parenting; Do What You Love
and Inspire Your Children!

A young person with a strong and powerful self-concept is even more important today than it has ever been before. Building the feelings of self worth whilst having fun colouring and repeating affirmations is a unique strategy for parents and child to bond and further develop attachment that is vital for building resilience, risk taking and future success. The mindfulness technique of quietly creating a beautiful visual while constantly seeing the words that have deep meaning enable a calmness in the young person and adult that is so necessary in the busy day to day life. This is just as important for the adult as it is for the child.

As a grandma and great aunty it will be wonderful to have another strategy to have meaningful time with each special young person in a calm relaxed atmosphere. I am grateful to Kylie for developing a resource that I can use to build that important bond with the important young people in my life.

Judy Hatswell
Registered Psychologist
Senior Faculty William Glasser Institute

Mindfulness colouring with affirmations for kids and adults gives you the opportunity to connect with your child by combining colouring with positive self-talk using affirmations.

Colouring is a mindfulness activity that you can do together to help you both unwind, de-stress, and relax. Just 10–20 minutes a day of colouring and reflecting on positive affirmations with your child gives them the gift of your undivided attention, while taking the opportunity to teach them the power of positive self-talk through affirmations. Children's confidence and self-worth thrive on adult attention. This chosen activity to "connect together" is also an opportunity to get off all devices, explore creativity together and enjoy the beauty of being in the present. These are the moments that count.

Mindfulness is all about focusing your thoughts in the moment that you are experiencing right now. Colouring will help you to develop your mindfulness skills by focusing completely on the present moment as you explore your own creativity. When you're calm and relaxed, it is the ideal time to embrace the positive statements in this book. Increasing mindfulness helps parents, carers and children to be less reactive and more aware of emotions while increasing concentration, memory and general wellbeing.

Affirmations are a proven method of building a healthy self-esteem and attracting abundance into your life. Similarly to exercise, affirmations create feel-good hormones and tune our brains to more positive thoughts. This brings about a happier state of mind while building a stronger belief in your own abilities. When we verbally affirm our dreams and ambitions, we are empowered with our own reassurance that our hopeful words will become a reality.

You are what you think. Teaching children to shut down any negative inner voice chatter and replace it with positive thoughts and words gives them the courage to believe in themselves and to take action to chase their hopes and dreams. It's a fun way for parents to teach children that affirmations can be used as "Magical Superpowers" to affirm self-worth and show that those who believe in themselves live happier lives.

Create **healthy habits** in children right from the start through the use of affirmations and positive self-talk. It's also a gentle reminder to all adults to believe in themselves too, while setting an example through your own positive self-talk, vital for kids to mirror.

The benefit of this book will be for you and your child to share instant feelings of gratitude, love and connection, positive thinking, focus and relaxation, while practising mindfulness and noticing the difference this brings to your day.

Put on some peaceful music or find a quiet spot outdoors while you colour and later refer to the back of this book for your own Affirmations and Gratitude Lists that both you and your child can fill in. Like anything, a habit is only formed when practised often.

With love and inspiration,

Kylie ♡ xx

This book belongs to

_____

I use this book to practice talking positively about myself and others.
My positive attitude brings me happiness.

Only I can control my feelings. I choose happiness.

I am loveable.
I am unique
and perfect
just the
way I am.

I am grateful for all that I have in my life right now. Good things happen when I am grateful.

I have courage and I am always kind.

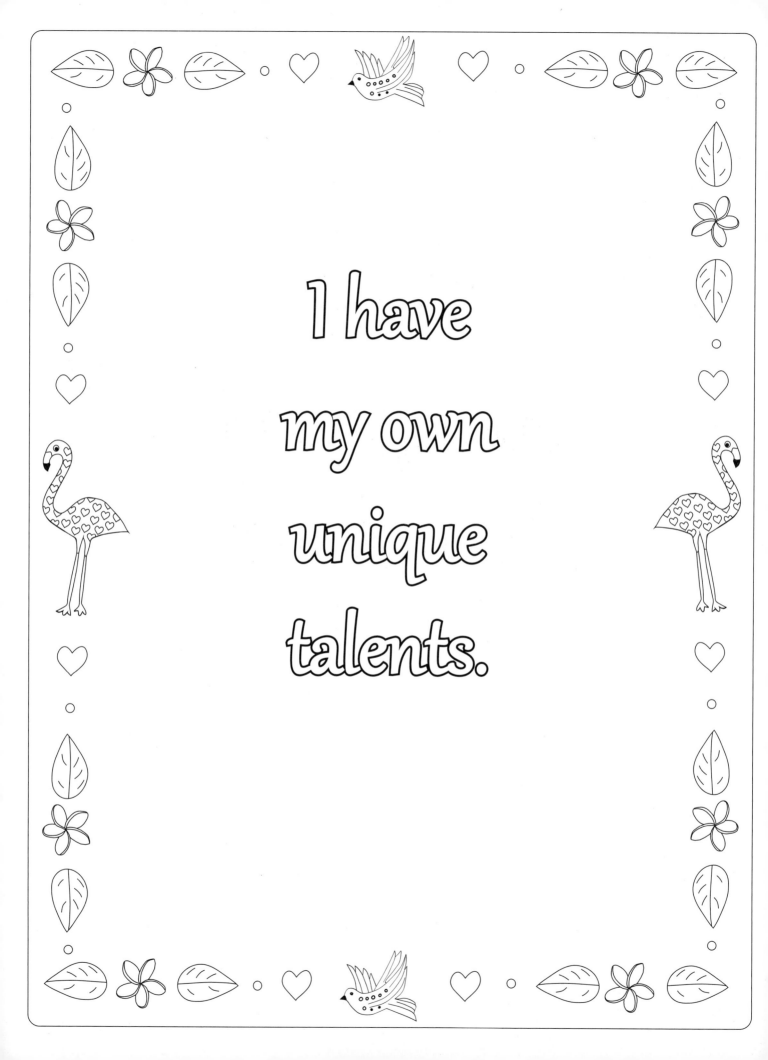

I have my own unique talents.

No dream is too big

I create
the life
I imagine.

I learn something every day.

I love
to learn.

We are
all unique.
I see the
best in
everyone.

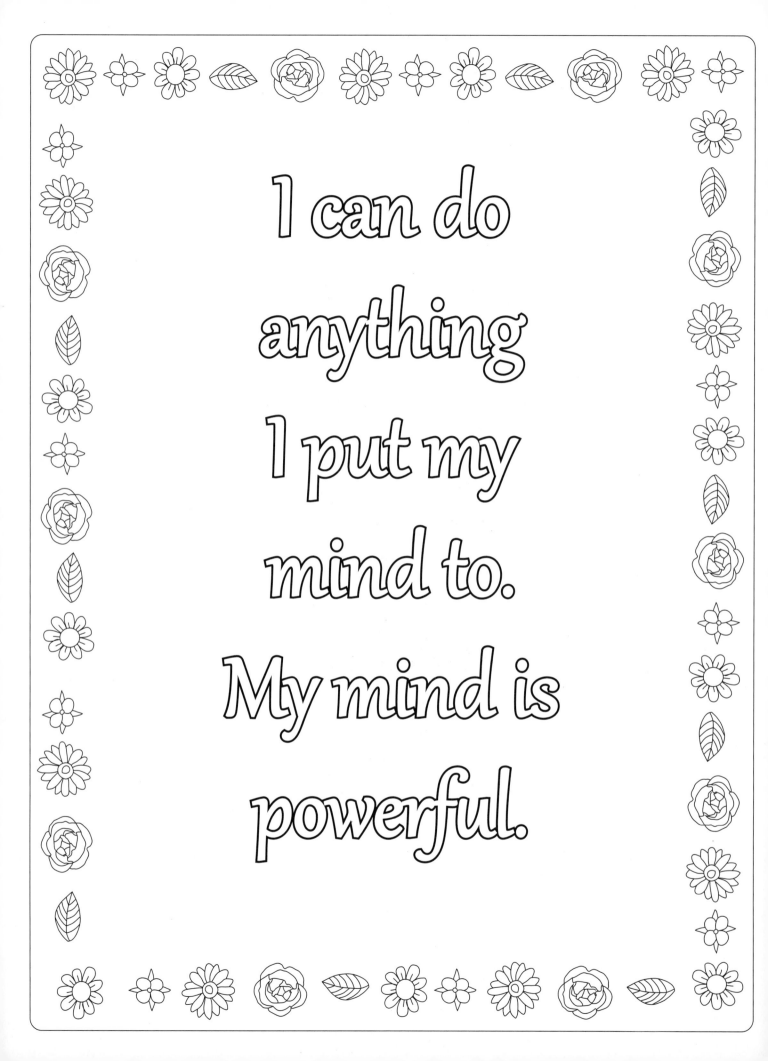

I think and speak positively.
My future is bright.

My family love and support me.

I never compare myself to others. We are all proudly unique and loveable.

Unique and Loveable

Friends

I admire and support my friends' achievements. They inspire me.

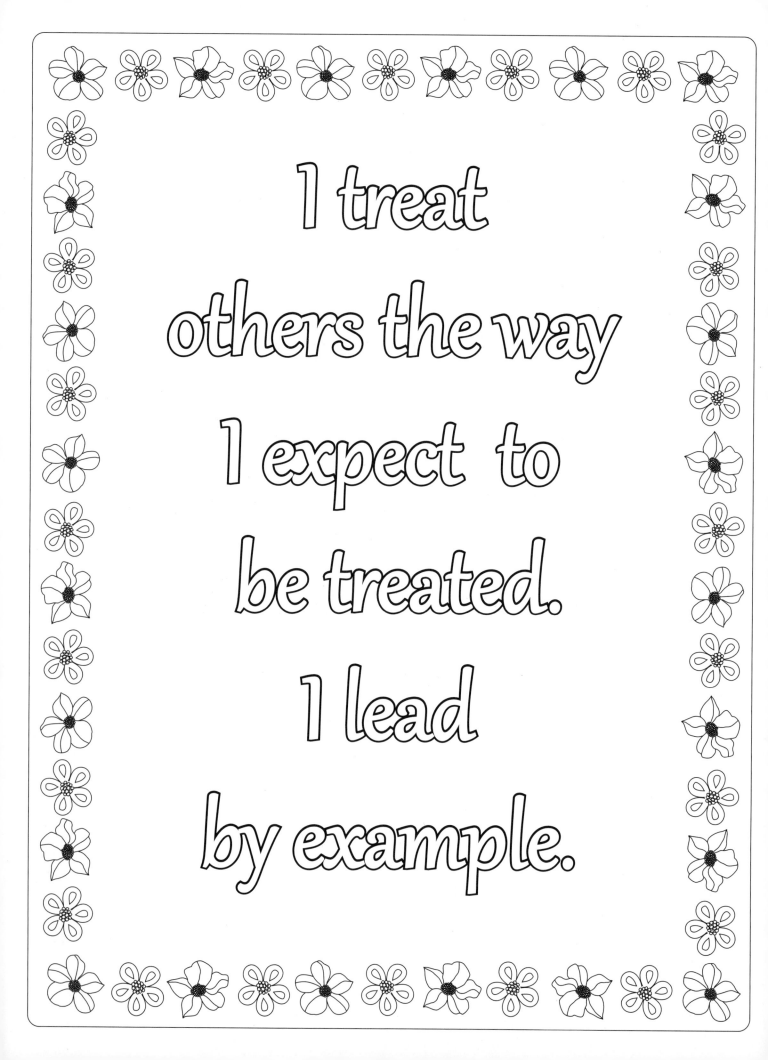

Kindness

I get back what I give.

I believe

in miracles.

I believe in myself. Determination makes my dreams come true.

I never give up and I always do my best.

Patience

My dreams are coming true.

I see all the good around me. I attract love, joy and happiness.

Love Joy Happiness

When I fill my heart with gratitude, I feel happy.

Happiness
is enjoying
the little
things.

always learning

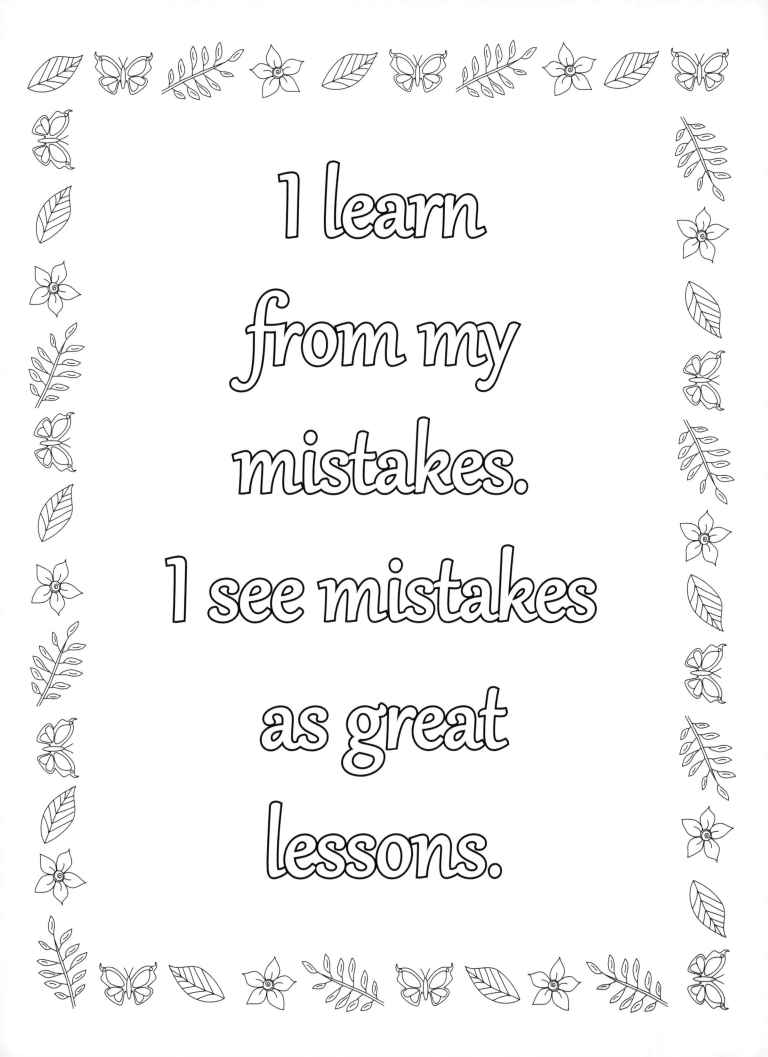

I learn from my mistakes. I see mistakes as great lessons.

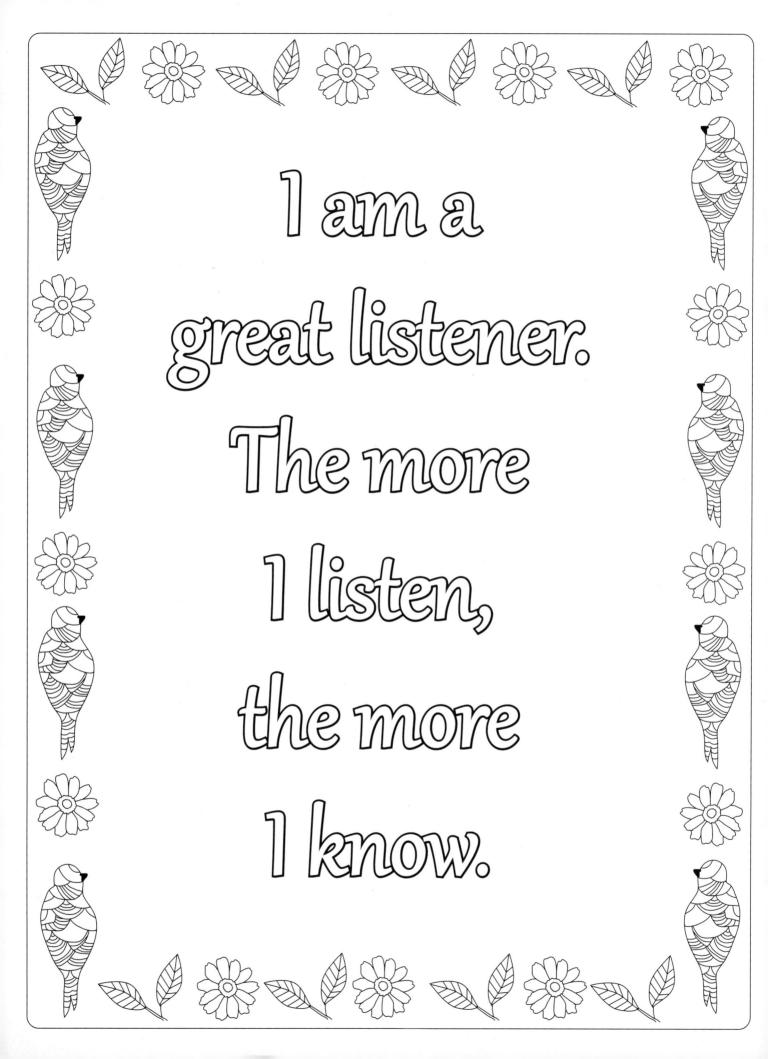

I am a
great listener.
The more
I listen,
the more
I know.

Love & Friendship

I listen because I care.

I accept
and
forgive
easily.

I am
creative
and have
a wild
imagination.

Creativity relaxes me.

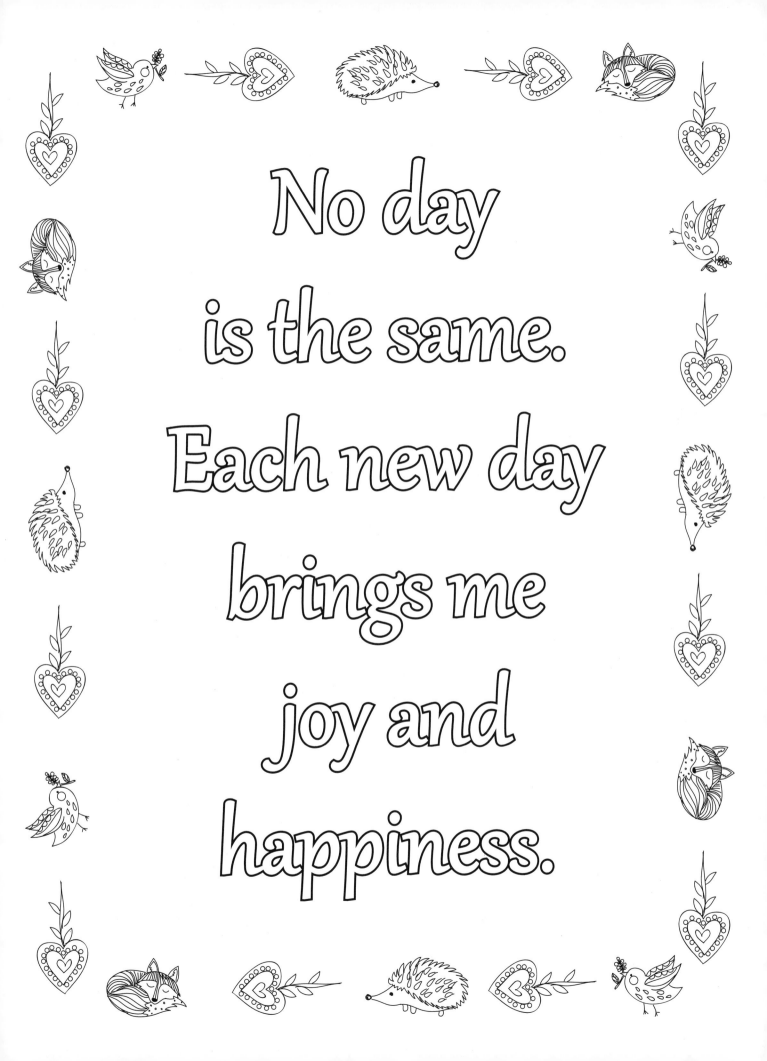

No day
is the same.
Each new day
brings me
joy and
happiness.

A smile is contagious. I see smiling faces all around me.

Honesty

I do what feels right for me.
I can say no gently.

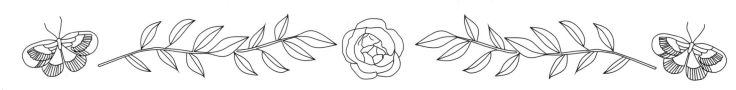

Positive thoughts bring happy feelings. I fill my mind with positive thoughts.

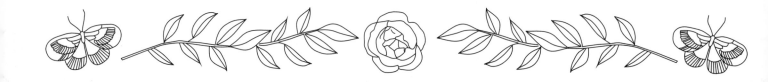

Music is my happy place.

Love
is all
I need.

My emotions come and go. I can handle anything.

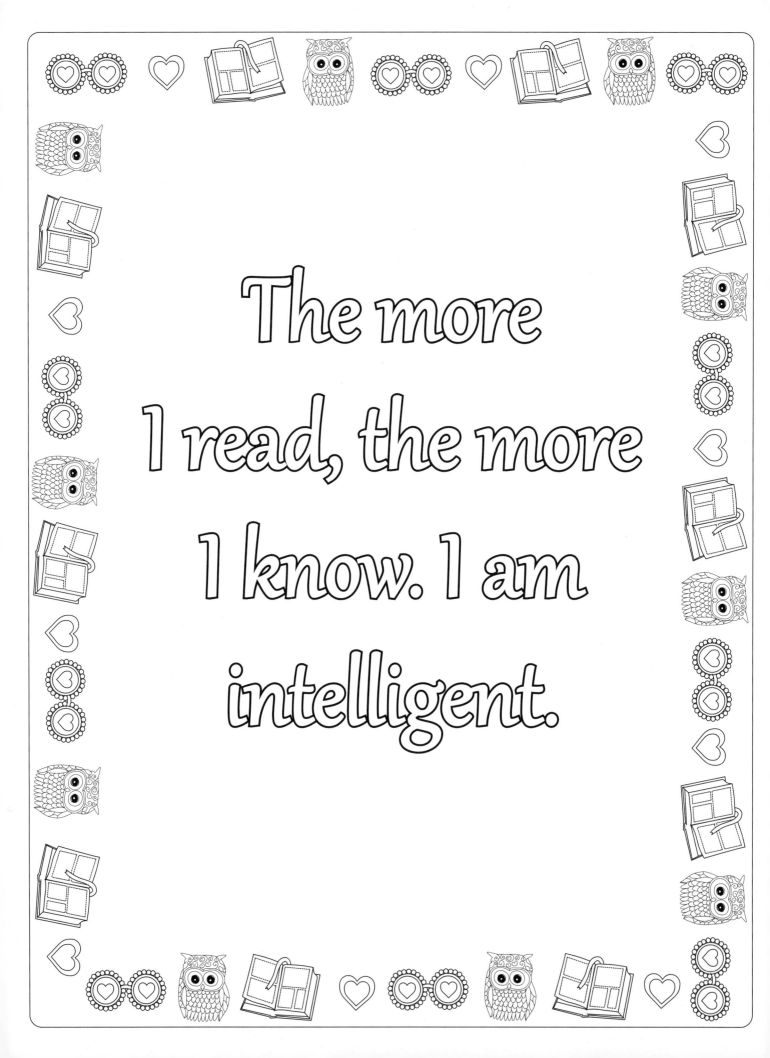

The more
I read, the more
I know. I am
intelligent.

I love to learn.

Love
and
Support

It is ok
to ask
for help.
I am never
alone.

I have courage and face my fears. This helps me grow. I am strong.

Courage

I can solve any problem. Challenges give me confidence.

I am confident in all that I do. I like to inspire others.

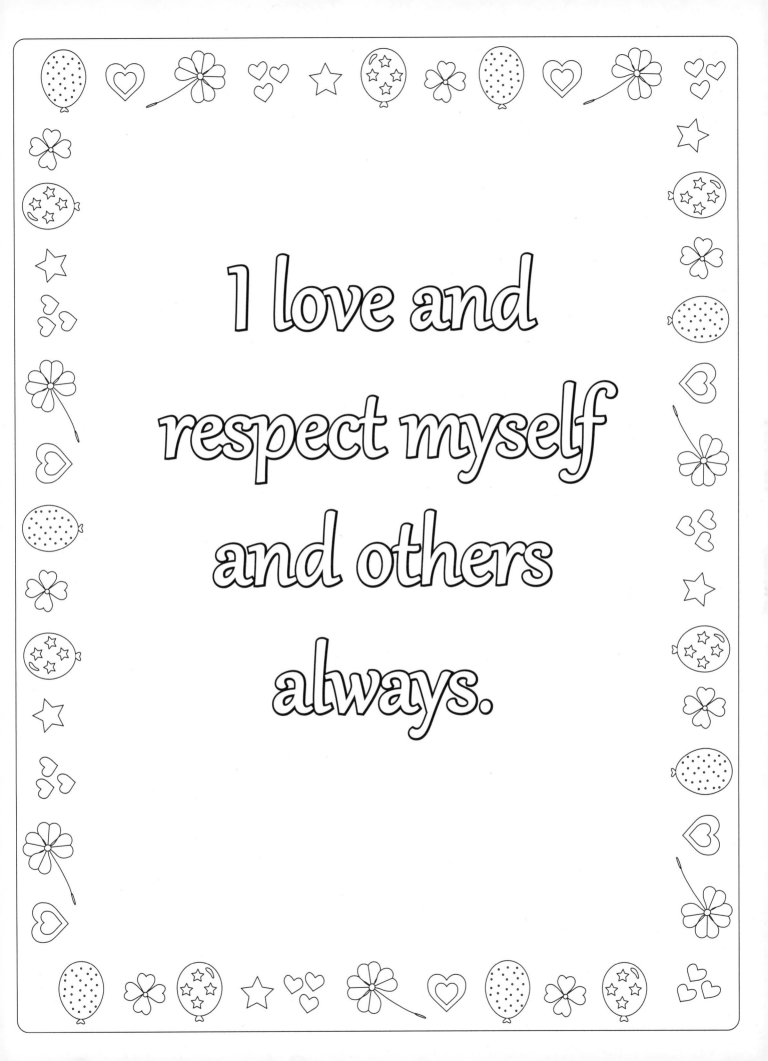

I love and
respect myself
and others
always.

It feels good to be generous and share.

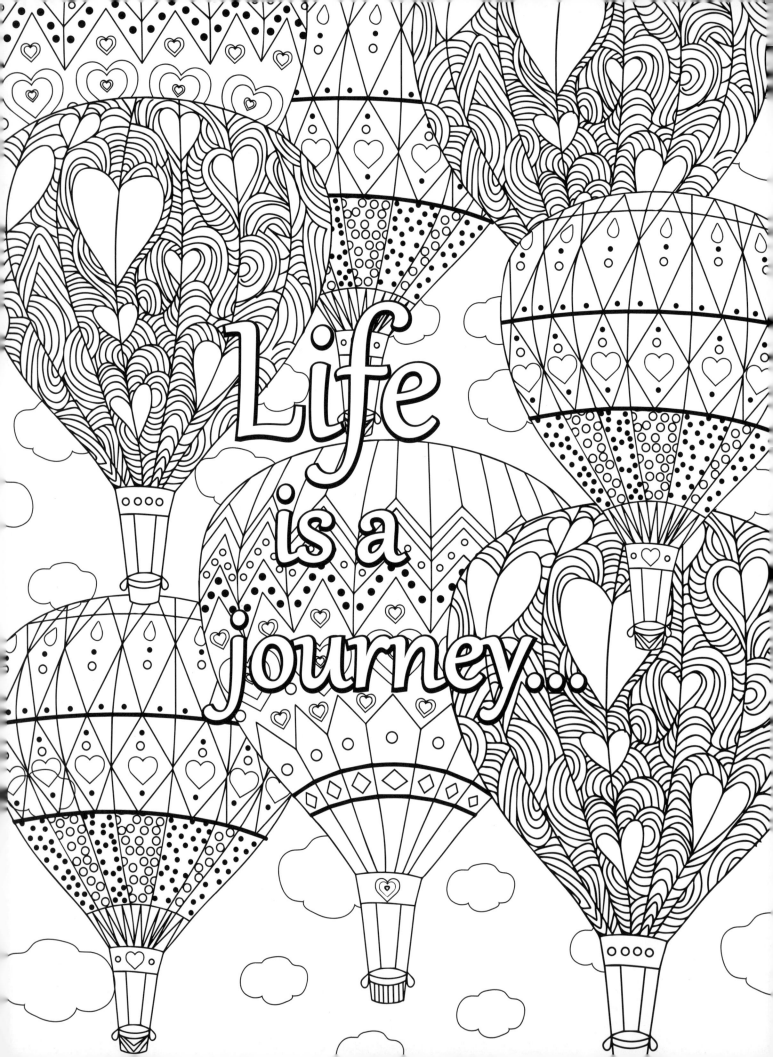

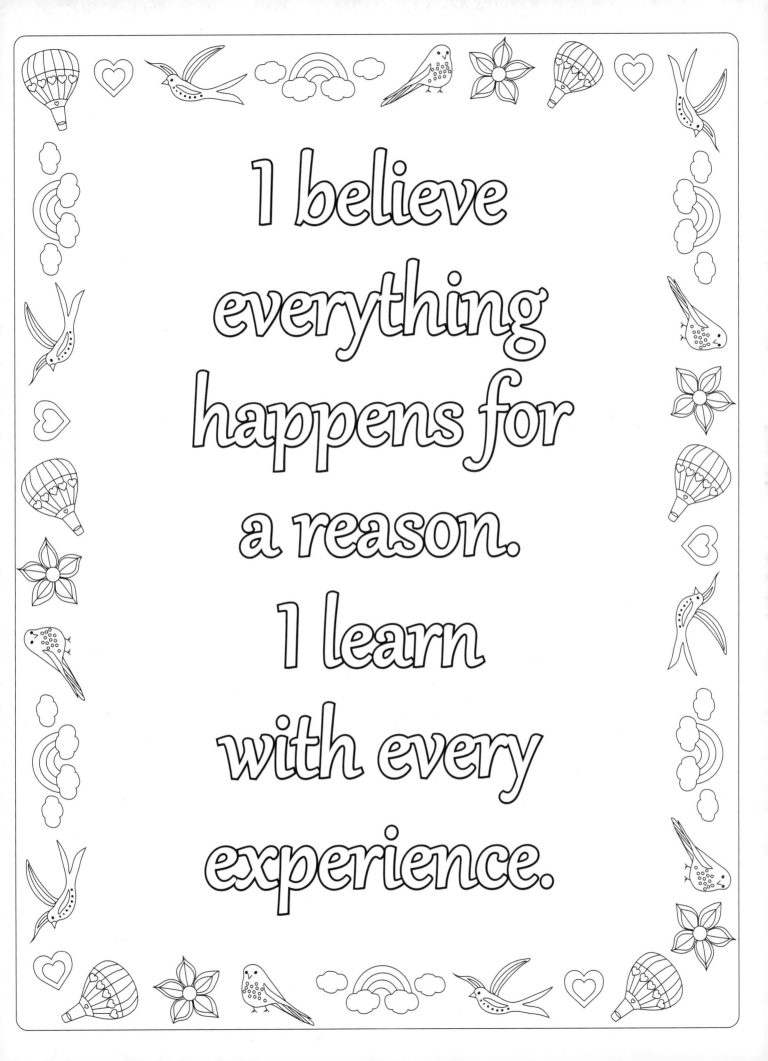

I believe everything happens for a reason. I learn with every experience.

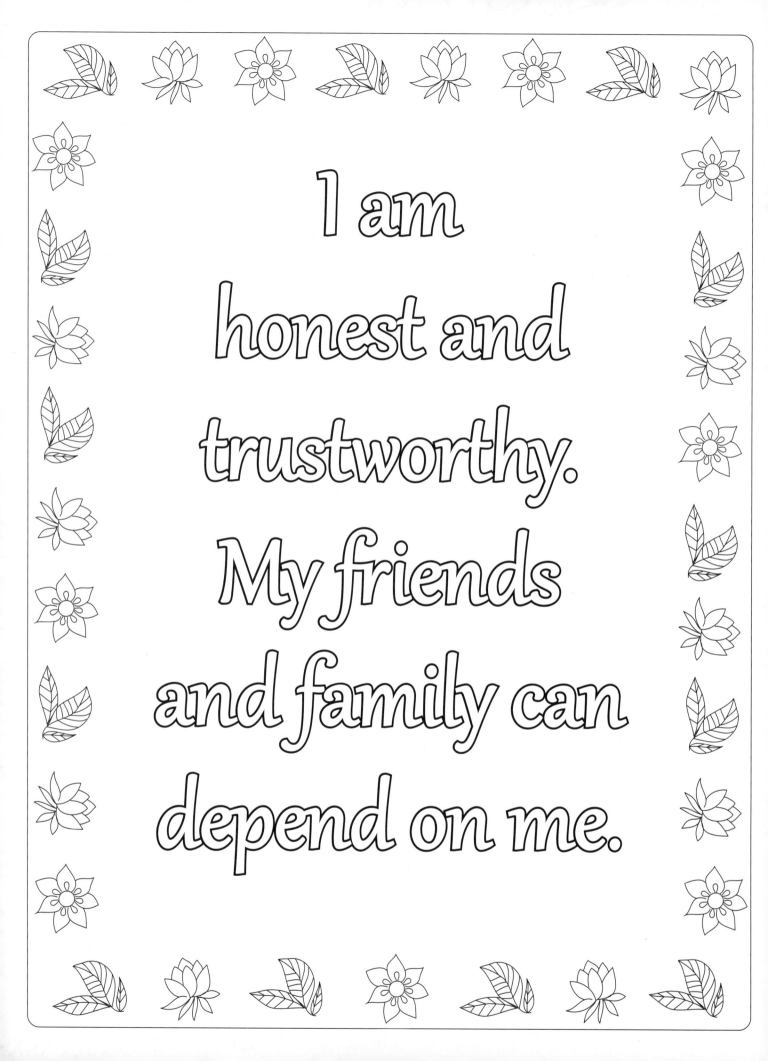

Honesty

I do more
of what makes
me happy.

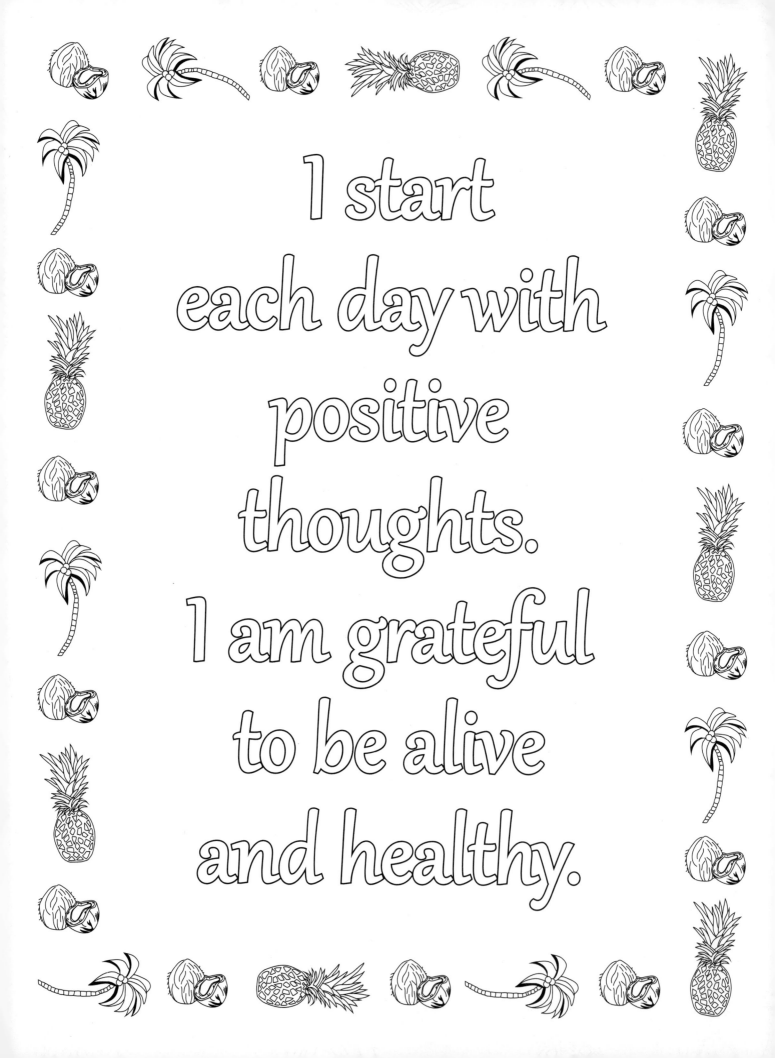

I start each day with positive thoughts. I am grateful to be alive and healthy.

I love life
and life
loves me.

Love
Live
Celebrate

It's my time to shine.

My list of affirmations
that I practise every day.

WISHES   HOPES   DREAMS

My future is bright.

I use this page to draw a dream and this is how it looks.

MY GRATITUDE LIST

My list of things to be grateful for that I reflect on every day.
This helps me when I'm feeling sad and brightens up my day.

"GRATITUDE IS MY NEW ATTITUDE"

Kylie resides by the seaside in a beautiful part of the world in Sydney, Australia. She loves being creative and is passionate about design, drawing and painting. It has always been in her nature to help those around her to see the bright side of life. Her strong desire to help others to look at the positives and live more in the present moment has led her to create her art and first colouring book.

She is thankful for every step of her life journey, including some challenges along the way, and appreciates the enlightenment and learning she has gained, particularly after becoming a mother to her beautiful daughter, Jasmin. While navigating her way through the loss of her marriage and her mother passing at the same time, she realised that creativity and positivity are the answers to stress and can place you on the path to healing.

Kylie is grateful to her late mother and grandmother for their infectious love, creative talents, and positive outlook, and to her father for his words of wisdom and unconditional support.

A long modelling career overseas and her love of travel strengthened her belief that "life does not have to be ordinary". Later, she designed a brand of kids clothing and décor called Meemini, based around inspirational messages to wear and share. She soon realised that when you discover what you're good at and have passion for, all you need to do is believe in yourself and let yourself evolve.

Kylie aims to encourage others to have awareness around their own thoughts and words and to realise the impact that positivity can have in their lives. Her hope is that adults can set a good example for little ones to mirror. She believes that being more mindful, especially around children, will bring about a much happier and healthier life. Her driving motivation is to be the best possible role model to Jasmin, so her daughter too will follow her dreams and find her life purpose.

Kylie's interest in psychology and how a person's childhood can shape their adult life, along with her own experiences, have compelled her to gain more knowledge from professionals in the areas of self-empowerment and wellbeing. She understood the full power of being present and more mindful while sharing creativity with her daughter. Their love and connection were strengthened through the experience, and Jasmin embraced the positive affirming messages, which reinforced Kylie's passion for this book.

Mindfulness colouring with affirmations for kids and adults has been designed for children and grown-ups to connect with each other using the combination of creativity and positivity as a daily mindfulness tool. This is Kylie's heartfelt gift to you and all the beautiful children out there who deserve the happiness that every parent wishes for them.